D1738080

Rosicrucian in the Basement

Rosicrucian in the Basement

Selected Poems

Robert Sward

Black Moss Press

2001

Published by Black Moss Press at 2450 Byng Road, Windsor, Ontario, N8W3E8. Black Moss books are distributed in Canada and the U.S. by Firefly Books, 3680 Victoria Park Ave., Willowdale, Ontario, Canada. All orders should be directed there.

Black Moss would like to acknowledge the support of the Canada Council for the Arts and the Ontario Arts Council for its publishing program.

National Library of Canada Cataloguing in Publication Data
Sward, Robert, 1933-
         Rosicrucian in the basement
Poems.
ISBN 0-88753-353-1
         I. Title.
PS8587.W35R68 2001   C811'.54   C2001-901866-5
PR9199.3.S937R68 2001

Acknowledgments

Grateful acknowledgment is made to the editors of the following publications for permission to reprint many of the poems in this book:
Alsop Review, Ambit (London, England), Another Chicago Magazine (ACM #37), Blue Moon Review, BookPress: The Newspaper of the Literary Arts (Ithaca, NY), Davka, Jewish Cultural Revolution (San Francisco), Disquieting Muses, Fiction-Online, Fiddlehead, Free Lunch, Hanging Loose Press, Mudlark, "Mudlark Poster #7," Paris Review, Podiatry Online Central, Poetry Magazine.com, QUARRY WEST #35, Anthology, RealPoetik (rpoetik), Salt Spring Island Tatler, Shirim, Santa Clara Review, SOLO, Web Del Sol MiniChap, X-CONNECT (CrossConnect)

*   *   *

Thanks to Allan Kornblum and Coffee House Press for permission to include "Hannah," "Nightgown, Wife's Gown" and "For My Son, Michael," which appeared in *Four Incarnations*.

*   *   *

With special thanks to Gloria, Elissa Alford, Jonathan Alford, Charles Atkinson, Ellen Bass, Rose Black, Robert Bly, Dr. Rachel Callaghan, Maria Elena Caballero-Robb, Ruth Daigon, Dion Farquhar, Dana Gioia, Heidi Alford Jones, Peter Gilford, James D. Houston, Dr. Ed Jackson, Coeleen Kiebert, Patrick McCarthy, Mort Marcus, Doug McClellan, William Minor, David Swanger, and Tilly Shaw.

Introduction

William Minor

The appearance of a new book of poems by Robert Sward is a significant event—one uncompromised by the place this book will eventually take in the already impressive body of work he has afforded his readers.

Rosicrucian in the Basement is of special significance for a poet whose mature work has been hailed by Carolyn Kizer as "fresh, ingenuous, and funnier than ever." The poet, with customary generosity, is offering a book so filled with love (enhanced by artistic skill) that this simple four-letter word is rendered fully plausible, accessible, redeemed. The problems that lesser practitioners too often fall into while addressing the topic—insincerity or self-aggrandizement—are simply not present here, and what we are left with is The Real Thing, in all its humble glory—not as an object apart, but the life of our life.

Robert Sward is also a master at: (1) astonishing long term fans, such as myself, with his ongoing capacity for variety and surprise; (2) presenting abstruse or complex concerns in a manner that is refreshingly straightforward, even simple, and (3) telling a story, providing a continuous narrative thread, yet remaining totally lyrical at the same time.

On the first count, Watch out! Although Robert is a proven, prolific, veteran performer, he has a way—like first-rate jazz improvisers—of keeping everybody on their toes. You're never quite sure just where he's going to go next, but when he gets there, the move—no matter how audacious at the time—was the right move: the result of seasoned versatility combined with a willingness to seek out new directions at considerable risk.

Not too long ago, I heard guitarist Bill Frisell at the Monterey Jazz Festival. I was surprised to find myself comparing the poems that make up Robert's book, which I had just read, with the work of this constantly evolving, incessantly surprising and delighting musician. Jazz critics have commented on Frisell's "unusual tonal colors," his playfulness and humor ("an eerie sense of funhouse mirrors"), his talent for surprise ("a Pandora's box of unexpected sounds and twisting mercurial lines"), and his ability to combine a laid-back, down home ("the happier strains of an American yesterday") approach with a totally contemporaneous sound ("tastefully minimal flashes of electronic sleight of hand"). I was tempted to borrow or steal such phrases of praise and apply them to Robert Sward's latest poems (and I just did!), for Robert, like Bill Frisell, has the unique ability to take us to some Great Good Place of his own devising, but one with a slight and occasionally fearful edge to it—keeping his readers (or listeners) constantly alert and alive.

Hearing Bill Frisell, I had a vision of my Arkansas father, no longer alive, speaking to me from whatever quarters he now inhabits, saying (and with the thick accent he never lost on earth and I'm sure he still retains), "Bill, I am pleased to see that at long last you have finally found some of that there jazz music that even I can appreciate!" And I can hear my father, having read Robert Sward's latest poems, saying the same thing about what he used to call "poultry." While on the surface they may not appear to have much in common, I think my father and the "father" of Robert's poems would get along quite well—just as the country-minimalism, or what one critic has called "porch music," of Bill Frisell is fully compatible with the podiatry-based wisdom of Robert's *Rosicrucian in the Basement.*

The ability to present highly complex concerns and insights in a straightforward, accessible manner—to create poems that grow increasingly "baroque" in their very economy (a trait the Japanese call "yugen," a preference for suggestion over overt statement)—is a gift that Robert Sward is willing to share with us in his new work—alongwith the third ingredient I mentioned: a nearly miraculous ability to blend straight narration and lyricism: to create a genre all his own that combines and transcends any cramped distinctions between prose and poetry. It's not an easy feat, technically or otherwise. When I try this in my own work, I tend to slip into what people regard as strictly prose (the "poetry," they say, drops out). Yet Robert somehow manages to juggle both worlds until they blur, blessedly, into a single form of continuous delight. The "characters" presented become indelible, as in fine fiction; the settings vivid in their detail, yet the "music" never stops—the poems filled as they are with infectious rhythms, touchstone phrases, and delectable juxtapositions.

So welcome to the amazing universe of Robert Sward, with all of its fresh and surprising twists and turns this time out: a world that probes more deeply (than perhaps it has dared to before) into the troublesome (and endlessly rewarding) terrain of metaphysics—eternity placed just where it should be, embedded in the here and now; the slightly demonic firmly rooted in the divine. Welcome to a set of philosophical and religious concerns that never lose sight of the all-too-human (and endlessly rewarding also) desire to delight and entertain. Above all, welcome to a world rife with love as it really is: teasing, tantalizing, torturous at times, yet full of infinite possibility and—if I may be permitted this phrase a third time—endlessly rewarding.

Be prepared to meet the whole "family," and to accept an invitation to step into their shoes. I guarantee you'll never forget the experience. "Too good for feet? Here, Son, try walking in these."

CONTENTS

I ROSICRUCIAN IN THE BASEMENT – A POEM CYCLE

ROSICRUCIAN IN THE BASEMENT   13
THE PODIATRIST'S SON   17
ONE-STOP FOOT SHOP   20
GOOD NEWS FROM THE OTHER WORLD   21
ARCH SUPPORTS–THE FITTING   23
GOD IS IN THE CRACKS   24
GOD'S PODIATRIST   25
WEDDING #2   26

II PORTRAIT OF AN L.A. DAUGHTER

PORTRAIT OF AN L.A. DAUGHTER   31
HANNAH   34
DANTE PARADISO, ACTRESS   35
TAKE ME HOME, I NEED REPAIR   37
WATER BREATHER: FOUR FOR MICHAEL   39

III FASHION MAKES THE HEART GROW FONDER

SEX & TV WITH AUNT MIRIAM – 1945   47
DICK IN THE DRAWER   52
MILLIONAIRE   53
THE BIGGEST PARTY ANIMAL OF THEM ALL   55
FASHION MAKES THE HEART GROW FONDER   58
MY MUSE   60
NIGHTGOWN, WIFE'S GOWN   62
AMNESIA   63
THE HOUSE ON STILTS   65
PRAYER FOR MY MOTHER   67

ROSICRUCIAN IN THE BASEMENT
A POEM CYCLE

"To a foot in a shoe, the whole world seems paved with leather."
—The Hitopadesa, c. 500 AD

1. Rosicrucian in the Basement

i.

"What's to explain?" he asks.

He's a closet meditator. Rosicrucian in the basement.

In my father's eyes: dream.

"There are two worlds," he says,

liquid-filled crystal flask

                    and yellow glass egg

on the altar.

He's the "professional man" —

            so she calls him, my stepmother.

That, and "the Doctor":

"The Doctor will see you now," she says,

            working as his receptionist.

He's podiatrist—foot surgery a specialty—

            on Chicago's North Side.

Russian-born Orthodox Jew

            with zaftig Polish wife, posh silvery white starlet

            Hilton Hotel hostess.

ii.

This is his secret.

This is where he goes when he's not making money.

The way to the other world is into the basement

and he can't live without this other world.

"If he has to, he has to," my stepmother shrugs.

Keeps door locked when he's not down there.

Keeps the door locked when he is.

"Two nuts in the mini-bar," she mutters, banging pots

            in the kitchen upstairs.

Anyway, she needs to protect the family.

"Jew overboard," she yells, banging dishes.

"Peasant!" he yells back.

iii.

"There are two worlds," he says lighting incense, "the seen

and the unseen, and she doesn't understand.

This is my treasure," he says,

lead cooking in an iron pan,
liquid darkness and some gold.
"Son, there are three souls: one, the Supernal;
        two, the concealed

                            female soul, soul like glue...
holds it all together..."
"And the third?" I ask.
We stand there: "I can't recall."
He begins to chant and wave incense.
No tallis, no yarmulke,
just knotty pine walls and mini-bar
        size of a ouija board,
a little schnapps and shot glasses
on the lower shelf,
and I'm no help.
Just back from seven thousand dollar trip,
four weeks with Swami Muktananda,

                                    thinking

Now there's someone who knew how to convert
the soul's longing into gold.
Father, my father: he has this emerald tablet
        with a single word written on it
and an arrow pointing.

2. Jesus

"What is it with the cross? You believe in Jesus, dad?"
"What?"
"Are you still a Jew?"
He turns away.
"Damnit, it's not a religion, *verstehst*?"
        Brings fist down on the altar.
 "We seek the perfection of metals," he says,
        re-lighting stove,
                "salvation by smelting."

"But what's the point?" I ask.

"The point? Internal alchemy, *shmegegge. Rosa mystica*," he shouts.

Meat into spirit, darkness into light."

Seated now, seated on bar stools.
Flickering candle in a windowless room.
Visible and invisible. Face of my father
            in the other world.
I see him, see him in me
my rosy cross
                    podiatrist father.
"I'm making no secret of this secret," he says,
turning to the altar.
"Tell me, tell me how to pray."
"Burst," he says, "burst like a star."

3. Rosy Cross Father

Mother:
"Yes, he still believes. Imagine—
            American Jews,
                    when they die,
roll underground for three days
to reach the Holy Land.
He believes that."

We're standing at the Rosicrucian mini-bar listening,
                    father
            with thick, dark-rimmed glasses
blue-denim shirt,
            bristly white mustache,
            and dome forehead.

"Your stepmother's on the phone with her sister," he says.

"He thinks he can look into the invisible,"
            she says from above.
"He thinks he can peek into the other world,
like God's out there waiting for him...
Meshugge!"

She starts the dishwasher.

"As above, so below," he says.
"I'm not so sure," I say.
"Listen, everyone's got some stink," he says,
        grabbing my arm,
                "you think you're immune?"
I shake my head.

"To look for God is to find Him," he says.
"If God lived on earth," she says, "people would knock out
        all His windows."
"Kibbitzer," he yells back. "Gottenyu! Shiksa brain!"

Father turns to his "apparatus,"
"visual scriptures," he calls them,
        tinctures and elixirs,
                the silvery dark and the silvery white.

"We of the here-and-now, pay our respects
to the invisible.
                Your soul is a soul," he says, turning to me,
"but body is a soul, too. As the poet says,
'we are the bees of the golden hive of the invisible.'"
"What poet, Dad?"
"The poet! Goddamnit, the poet," he yells.

He's seventy-one, paler these days, showing more forehead,
        thinning down.

"We live in darkness and it looks like light.
Now listen to me: I'm unhooking from the world, understand?
Everything is a covering,
contains its opposite.
The demonic is rooted in the divine.
Son, you're an Outside," he says,
        "waiting for an Inside.
but I want you to know..."
"Know what, Dad?"
"I'm gonna keep a place for you in the other world."

16   Robert Sward

THE PODIATRIST'S SON

"When our feet hurt, we hurt all over."
            –Socrates

1. The Podiatrist's Son

Mother:
"One day the kid will wake up,
            come down to earth
and enroll
            at the Illinois College of Podiatry."

                        Father:
                        "But look, his feet aren't on the ground."

"They've never been on the ground. He's a dreamer."

                        "Just look at that posture! And he toes in.
                        Poor feet, poor posture.
                        The boy lives in another world."

"Wait, I think he needs a new pair of shoes."

                        "Oxfords, shoes that will support him,
                        shoes with laces,
                        shoes that breathe."

"Listen. Listen to your father," she says.

2. How To Shop For Shoes

                        "No loafers, no sandals, nothing
                        without laces," he says.

                        "There are fifty-two bones in the feet;
                        thirty-three joints; more than one hundred
                        tendons, muscles and ligaments..."

We're on our way to Jackson's Shoes.

"Fit for length, fit for width,
get both feet fitted.

"People are asymmetrical. You'll find
one foot, one testicle, one breast
larger than the other..."

"Listen, listen to your father," she says.

"Feet swell, grow larger
as the day goes on.

"So, nu? shop when they're bigger,
shop for the larger foot.

"Otherwise...
heel pain, heel spurs, bunions and hammertoes...

"Remember, there's no break in period,
shoes don't break in.
Buy what feels right now."

"Listen, listen to your father."

3. *Getting Through the Night*

"So: the foot is the mirror of health.
What's that smell?
Let me see your feet. Oi!

"How many times do I have to say it?
A pair of feet have twenty-five thousand
sweat glands, can produce eight ounces,
a cup of perspiration in a single day.

"One quarter of all the bones in the human body
are in the feet."

He sits at my bedside carving arch supports.

"Take a flashlight.
Never walk around in the dark.
Most foot fractures occur at night...

"Now remember your slippers," he says
as I head for the bathroom.

In my father's house
there are no bedtime stories.

ONE-STOP FOOT SHOP

"We walk with angels
and they are our feet.

"'Vibrating energy packets,'" he calls them. "'Bundles of soul
in a world of meat.' Early warning system—
                              dry skin and brittle nails;
feelings of numbness and cold;
these are symptoms; they mean something.
I see things physicians miss.

"All you have to do is open your eyes, just open your eyes,
and you'll see: seven-eighths of everything is invisible, a spirit
inside the spirit.
The soul is rooted in the foot.
As your friend Bly says, 'The soul longs to go down';
feet know the way to the other world,
that world where people are awake.
So do me a favor: dream me no dreams.
A dreamer is someone who's asleep.

"You know, the material world is infinite,
but boring infinite," he says, cigarette in hand,
little wings fluttering at his ankles.

"And women," he says, smacking his head,
"four times as many foot problems as men.
High heels are the culprit.

"I may be a podiatrist, but I know what I'm about:
feet. Feet don't lie,
            don't cheat, don't kiss ass. Truth is,
peoples' feet are too good for them.

GOOD NEWS FROM THE OTHER WORLD

Palm Springs, CA

"Dad, you're lookin' good," I say,
"like the fountain of youth."

His hands on my feet, grimacing, weary,
mercurial, wing-footed
eighty-year-old doctor.

Wears a denim shirt, bola tie,
turquoise and silver tip,
tanned, tennis-playing, macho...

"Making more money now,
more than in Skokie.
But you need arch supports," he says,
encasing my feet in plaster.

Damaged feet. Feet out of alignment.
Four-times married, forty-year-old feet.

"Well, good news from the other world," he says.

"Really?"

"The void is nothing but people's breath."

"So something survives?" I say.

"Feet survive. Feet and breath survive," he says,
"peoples' feet and peoples' breath."

"That is good news," I say.

"Don't mock me," he says.
"Do you know you still 'toe in'?
That your head 'pitches forward'?
You're past the half-way mark, son.

God is not altruistic, you know,
He doesn't make exceptions.
Of course things are dark and light at once."

Huh? Who is he? Whoever was my father?

Bloodied in some Russian pogrom.
Nixon-lover on the North Side of Chicago.
Blue denim, bola tie Republican.

Rosicrucian cowboy in the Promised Land.

GOD'S PODIATRIST

Palm Springs, CA

Corns, calluses, pain
      in the joints of my toes.
Masked man in the half light,
starched white jacket and pants,
      shaking his head.
"Dad, what are you doing?"
 "Re-fitting the supports.
What is it with you?" he asks,
"Why don't you respond?
I've never seen such feet.
With a word, the world came into being," he murmurs,
cigarette in hand.
"With you, with arch supports even
      there are these feet that go nowhere.
Anyway, there's just one person,
God, God's body," he says.
"God has a body?" I ask.
"Of course he has a body, and feet."
"Feet?"
"Feet, of course feet.
You know he's not one to ask for help."
      Throws me my shoes. "You're finished."
"Help?" I ask.
"It's the least I can do," he says.
"You're a podiatrist for God?" I ask.
"Varicose veins.
The aroma of infinity.
feet sparking,   feet an endless ocean,
      feet made of music.
Of course I have to sort out foot from hallucination.
You can't treat a halo.
Don't look at me like that.
You're the one who doesn't respond to treatment.
God has feet like anyone else. You know it and I know it."
"I am that I am," I say.
"Says you," says my father.
"He is that he is and I'm his podiatrist.
What a son," he says.

WEDDING #2

i.

Temple Parking Lot

My father says:
"So, my son is getting married!"

"For the second time, dad."

"Yes, but weddings heal. The Talmud says
a wedding frees bride and groom
          from all past transgressions.
A wedding fixes all that's broken."

"You mean one marriage can fix another?" I ask,
          parking the old Plymouth.

He grabs my arm: "A happy marriage
gives eternal dispensation."

His eyes gather light.
"The Talmud says intercourse is one-sixtieth
the pleasure of paradise."

I'm wearing five-eyelet Florsheims
          with new arch supports.

"This is good." He waves to friends.
"Just don't fumble the goblet."

"The goblet?"

"The goblet you break after the vows.
This time use your heel. Smash it on the first try.
People'll be watching. Miss it and they'll laugh—
          like last time.
Don't fumble the goblet."

ii.

Temple Steps

Leads with his chin.
Visible and invisible.
Chin trembling, his face shining.

"I was an orphan."

"Yes, I know, dad."

"Did you know an orphan's dead parents are able to attend the wedding?"

"But dad, I'm not an orphan."

"Well, I just want you to know if you were,
                    we'd come anyway.
You know, your grandparents will be there too."

"How will they manage that?"

"What are you asking? They'll manage.
These are your grandparents:
Grandpa Hyman. Grandmother Bessie.
It's a tradition. The Talmud says.
If they have their bodies, they'll come with their bodies."

"But they're dead."

"So, they'll come without."

iii.

Temple Washroom

"When a man unites with his wife,
God is between them.
I'm telling you: lovemaking is ceremony.
The Talmud says.

You, you're not holy, but your wife is.
With her
          you go to a world outside the world."

"So?"

"So wash your hands before
          not after.
Wash for the pure and holy bride."

"But what about hygiene?"

"How did I bring you up?
Shame on you.
The socks come off and you make love.
The Talmud says. And you make her happy.
Schtepp. Schtepp. Do you understand?
Forget hygiene!
This is the pure and holy bride."

PORTRAIT OF AN L.A. DAUGHTER

"The Family is the Country of the Heart."

–Guiseppe Massini, Italian nationalist leader

PORTRAIT OF AN L.A. DAUGHTER

Take #1

Braided blonde hair
white and pink barrettes
Bette Davis gorgeous
I hug her
dreamy daughter with no make-up
silver skull and crossbones
middle
       finger
               ring
three or four others in each ear
rings in her navel
rings on her thumbs
gentle moonchild
       "pal" she announces
to "Porno for Pyros"
formerly the group "Jane's Addiction"
 "Nothing's Shocking"
with Perry Farrell
Dave Navarro on guitar
and Stephen Perkins
on drums
"Ain't No Right" they sing.
"What are you,
       some kind of groupy?" I ask.
She says nothing.
      Just turns up the volume.
"Been Caught Stealing"
      they sing.

I hold her
Wet 'n' Wild lip gloss
diamond stud earrings
and glitter on her cheeks

Wan, she's looking wan
my dancing daughter

Hannah Davi –a new name–
walk-on in the movie "Day Of Atonement"
      with Christopher Walken

And a part in a Levitz Furniture ad
      ("it's work")
and a part in an MCI commercial
      ("Best Friends")
breaking in
"Brotherhood Of Justice"

a Swiss Alps bar-maid
("classic blonde Gretel")
in a Folger's Coffee commercial

"Grunge is in" she says
visiting Santa Cruz
"any Goodwills around?"

*   *   *

Flashback

Appearing,
      "crowning" says the doctor

"Hannah" says her mother
"the name means 'grace'"

Two-year-old drooling
as I toss her into space
and back
      she falls
and back
into space again

Flawless teeth and perfect smile
one blue eye slightly larger than the other
her three thousand miles away mother
still present as
two as one
two breathing together
we three breathe again as one
Hannah O Hannah

HANNAH

Her third eye is strawberry jam
has a little iris in it
her eyelids
         are red
she's sleepy
         and the milk
         has gone down
         the wrong way.
I've just had breakfast
with the smallest person in the world.

DANTE PARADISO, ACTRESS

White, eight-door, hot tub
      limo behind us   the driver
      on his horn

Move, dammit, move! he yells. No green light,
       no green arrow,
no green anything.

"I love L.A. traffic because it means
a whole lot of other people are here too."

She's half way into the intersection
waiting to make a left turn

                         against

Four lanes of oncoming DeVilles.
      "L.A.'s famous for this. I love
how huge it is," she says,

"seeing strangers I'll never see again. And the restaurants...
and the guys...
              I should have been born here.
Anyway, I corrected the problem."

          Dante Paradiso,
                   the original
Miss Fire Cracker. Youngest, Newest, Freshest
Ingenue.

Part in "Show Girls" (ugh!),
part—dancer—in "Forrest Gump."

She is the sun and the moon.
Miss Gold Ring.

Applies Creme d'Elegance. "It tones the skin."
A little eyeliner,

Maybelline "tres noir."

"Look, look, there's Julia Roberts! See,
behind us."

Ms. Paradiso's the moon wearing make-up,
the sun reaching for blue eye-shadow,

      luminous,
            yellow, aqua beige and blue,

     the sky whitening,

turning, turning at last
pulling away from Ms. Roberts

     silicon limousine with a ready smile,

sunlight, sunlight, the Next Big Thing.

          —Los Angeles, 1999

TAKE ME HOME, I NEED REPAIR

"Take me home, I need repair. Take me please to anywhere."
—The Red Hot Chili Peppers

For my son, Nicholas

He's a musician
   prophet
      a raging Apollo
gold hoops,
   diamond stud earrings
toenails and fingernails
        painted black

6'3", 200 pounds
legs propped up
on a wobbly stool

      Listening
Magic-Red-Blood-Hot-Sugar
   Chili-Sex

What I see is insanity.
Whatever happened to humanity?

"Good lyrics," I say

"The Chili Peppers," he says
"it's rap and it sucks.
Actually, I like Punk more—"

White steel guitar in hand
he demonstrates:

Fuck you... he sings.
End of demonstration.

Now he's Anthony Keidis
a tube sock

on his dick
One hot minute, and I'm in it...

Next he's trancey, anguished
Sonic Youth

Later:

Washing windows,
scrubbing floors,
            dancing
doing
            standup
                        impressions

My son the genie
my son Mr. Clean

Tries to jump into my arms.
Where do kids come from anyway?

                  "Fucking life
                  Everything sucks," he says

Mourning Kurt Cobain,
            Hillel Slovak and the others
overdose dead.

Youthanasia

Whip-smart

Funk Da World
Funk Da World

I'm the father, I'm supposed to tell him—what?

"I know the truth," he says,
"I know the truth."

WATER BREATHER: FOUR FOR MICHAEL

1.

SWIMMER IN AIR

Gulper of sea,
swimmer in air,

he dives, dives in again
again
        water's
                water,
air is air.

"Water's
                water,
air is air,"
      I say.
"No," he says, "no."

He's the breather of water,
three-year-old refuser,
            won't be taught.

Intent, he makes his run,
big feet slapping, loopy leap
and sinks
        to the bottom.

Swim to him.

"Water's
                    water," I begin...
he's red-eyed, sputtering, shaking—
Clambers up the ladder
                 to the dock
                          and jumps.

Scoop and hug him close

                                        hold him out.

"Stroke, stroke
                inhale

                        in air

exhale in water," I say,

                                "like this, Michael.

Breathe in air,

                swim in water."

"No," he says, "no."

Slap, slap his feet
on the side of the dock

He breathes in water
and swims in the air

breathes in water
and swims in air.

2.
JULY 4

                "A boy achieves maximum pissing power at age 5 or 6...."
                                        —Dr. Ed Jackson

"Michael, what the—"

six-year-old, dick in hand,
turning, his stream unbroken,

nine feet if it's an inch,
                laughing, the kid's laughing
as he circles

360-degrees
hand all the time on the throttle,

slowly, back arched

he stands
       "Dick, dink, decker,
        weener, peter, pecker..." he sings
crowd gathering

nine feet from VW rooftop
to raging Mr. Beer-In-His-Hand.
"Is that your kid up there?"

I should laugh,
       get up there with him,
lead our friends in applause.

       "Dick, dink, decker," he sings,
face shining, joy to the world.

Rein him in, *do something,*
Jesus K. Christ,

"Dance," I want to say, "dance
on the roof of the German machine.

"Piss on, piss all you want—
What a stream!" I want to say.

Old fool, old scold,
too fearful to sing
"O Stream of Gold..."

Fucked father, fucked-up father,
I spank him instead.

3.
HOUSE BOAT
Lasqueti Islands, B.C.

Washing dishes in the darkness
with a hose,
I spray off the few
      remnants
of spaghetti onto the oysters

In their beds below.
Inside the single room
there is no running water—
      only the green hose
on the deck of our floating home.

We secure the lines,
bathe and sing, *We all live in a Yellow Submarine...*
I reach out in the darkness
hearing my son brushing his teeth
to borrow his toothbrush.

I cannot find my own:
Tasting
      my fourteen-year-old son's
mouth inside my mouth.
Then we find more dishes

And, as the moon rises and the lines
      go tight,
continue scrubbing and drying silverware
and plates,
      two dishwashers reading Braille.

4.

MOUNTAIN SOLITAIRE

i.

Jerome, Arizona

He's thirty-two, my age
when he was born.
Haven't seen him for four years,
estranged son of estranged wife.

Phone:
            "Please... leave... message..."
                        says the machine.
"Hey, Michael... It's Dad!"
He won't pick up, won't call back.

I court him, send gifts:
            "Oh, boy, a cordless phone
from, let's see now, Mr. Walk-around...
my much-doodling daddy!"

I see him shake his head.
And write, I write him a poem.
Read it onto his answering machine.
            "Dick, dink, decker,
                weener, peter, pecker..."

He's away —a girlfriend
plays back the message.
"There's a stalker..." she tells him.
"No, that's my father," he says,
and calls me. He likes the poem.

ii.

Golden Gate Park

We meet and he leads me
to the Hall of Flowers,
his dark hair combed forward,
bushing out over his ears,
           single white strand glinting in the sun.

He's three, six and thirty-two;
I'm thirty-two, thirty-eight and sixty-four.
The prodigal father
           and the abandoned 'live alone,'
Mr. Mountain Solitaire.

We stroll through the Garden of Fragrance,
oasis of lakes.
                    Absentee father
fathering,

he the fathered, fatherless
hungering

           son to be a father
           father to be father

This is the hunger.

                    —San Francisco, 1998

FASHION MAKES THE HEART GROW FONDER

"Give me no gold.
Give me no silver.
Give me paper. "
                                    –Jewish prayer

SEX & TV WITH AUNT MIRIAM – 1945

Part 1

"Always wash your hands after you've played in the backyard with those leaves and things before touching yourself," said my aunt, beginning our affair with this public service announcement.

"Yes, m'am."

"Eddie, I'm going to show you how broadminded I am."

"Okay."

"But first I want you to tell me what you do with Lenore and her sister."

"Nuthin."

"You spin the bottle?"

"Yeah."

Luminous brown-eyed English Miriam abuzz with heat,
My left arm around her, my right hand
in her right hand
       "Kiss me   love me   feel me, Eddie..."

I'm a pleaser. But... what was it she wanted me to do?

                        A seventh grader, I'd been held
back a year at school. "He tries hard, and he's smart about some things,
but..."Anyway, I was right in there for a while with the slow learners.

Four thousand feet down in a North of England coal mine,
I'd just have grabbed a shovel and gotten to work.
I'd have known right away what to do.

Holding me with one hand,
marking with the other,

D-I-C-K, wrote my twenty-something aunt.
Hmm. It felt good.

She finished by drawing some arrows and a bull's eye on her own body.

What was it like? It was like television, "informative and entertaining."
Never to have been fucked and never to have watched television either,
and then to be fucking and watching the evening news
on one of the first TVs in Chicago, and the Atomic
Bomb going off and the war over all at the same time, I think...
the truth is, I still don't understand.

The diagrams and the lettering helped.
I like seeing things labeled.
I'm so grateful.

"All art aspires to the state of music." That's true. I know that. And even at
thirteen I loved Gershwin ("Rhapsody in Blue"), but I knew real music when
I heard it. "O do me, thrill me." And that's what I went for. That's what I
learned at thirteen. And that's what I'm grateful for.

O Miriam, say it again. Tell me where you want it. Draw me a picture.
Ah, dearest, how helpful it's been having those letters printed on my dick.

                              How many times have I been told,
"Eddie, you don't know your ass from a hole in the ground"? More times
than there are stars in the sky. And I hold my head high. At least I know
where, O Aunt Miriam, O Miriam, to look for my dick.

*   *   *

Part 2

Fifty-two years later
"Oh, my God! I can't stand it," she said, hearing my voice.
"How are you, Eddie? I've been trying to find you. You're
a missing person, you know?"

"I write, I've even published," I said.

"I talked to that publisher of yours. Famous you're not."

"I know, I know. And what about you, Miriam?"

"I got some health problems. I go to temple, the B'nai Brith."

"And Uncle Jerry?"

"Dead. That's why I'm calling, Eddie. He's dead. Fifty-four years
we'd been together." Uncle Jerry, the handsomest man in Chicago,
circa 1945, singer on Chicago's WGN Radio.

"No one thought it would work. Fifty-four years and we yelled all
the time. What does anyone know about anything?"

"You stuck it out," I say. "That's good."

> She's twenty-one, twenty-two,
> pale, pinkie-brown where I put my lips.
>
> "Enjoy yourself, Eddie. Life is to enjoy."
> "What about Jerry? What about Uncle Jerry?"
>
>
> "Listen to me. People go up and back between loving
> and not loving.
> Do you understand, Eddie?"

My lips here, there...
                    She's teaching me. "This is how you do it."

                    "See," she says, "see."
                    I'm thirteen and not wanting to. Then
                    wanting.

                    "I want to."

"Woof, woof."

"That's Koko. That dog has a weight problem.
"She doesn't want to move.
"so I let her sleep on our bed.
"Koko is on morphine."

"Your dog is on morphine?"

"Did you ever hear of such a thing?
"Listen, you're all I got, Eddie.
"you're all the family that's left."

She wants me to fly to Chicago to see her.
"Do I have to draw you a picture?
"Come, Eddie. Come and see the sights."

                    We lie together... Betty Grable mouth
                    and red red lipstick
                    watching some old movie.
                    Listening at the same time to the radio.
                    It's the second half of a doubleheader.
                    Cubs versus the Pirates,
                    and the Cubs are ahead 4-3.

                    "That's good, Eddie. That's good.
                    "It's *The Star Spangled Banner*,
                    "O God, don't stop,

"It's The Stars and Stripes Forever.
"The Battle Hymn of the Republic.
"God Save the Queen!
"Do you understand?
"Don't stop."

She's pushing eighty, she says, and sells Avon. "It's a living."

I'm grateful, I want to say. I'm grateful for the arrows.
Whatever else has changed, I will always remember.

The aurora borealis,
and dawn's early light.
That was the year the Cubs won the pennant.

I understand, Miriam, these are the ties that bind.
Broad stripes and bright stars.
America the beautiful.
Purple mountains and spacious skies,
the screwed and sweetly screwy,
this our family, and this our country,

sweet land of liberty,
O fruited plain, O amber fields of grain,
from your apartment house to ours
('til Mom found out)
of thee, O darling, of thee I sing.

DICK IN THE DRAWER

What his dick was doing
in that dresser drawer
I have no idea,

Mom and Dad
            getting dressed or undressed,

she must have closed it
just shut it bang! without looking,

"Damnit!"
                    "O my God! O no!"

his schlong
            half in,
                                half out

of that bonnet top highboy,
wedding gift from Grandpa.

This time he doesn't whack her or get angry.

"I'll bandage it," she offers.

Ten year old in the next room,
I hear what I hear

"No," he says, his voice softening,
and again she offers,

"Filet of sole," she whispers, "jelly roll,
shimmy up the Maypole.

"Flag pole, peep hole..."
something about a camisole.

Home again, whole again
Mom and Dad again,
back in bed again.

MILLIONAIRE

—Grandpa Max, 1860-1958

1. *His inventions*

Born in 1860, Austro-Hungarian immigrant,
inventor of a cap to keep the fizz
in seltzer bottles, a refinement to the machine gun,
and a metal Rube Goldberg bookmark
            sold with a diagram and user manual,
Grandpa made big money speculating,
buying and selling tenements.
In the 1920s, offered stock in a start-up selling
flavored water and cocaine, he turned it down. "Coca Cola," he spat.
"Vhat dreck! Who'd buy?"

2. *His economies*

Lean, stiff-necked, pack-a-day smoker
with a fondness for syrupy wine, he wouldn't own a car,
used public transportation;
and, rather than buy toilet paper,
blackened his ass with yesterday's "Chicago Tribune."

Grandpa never left a restaurant
—"vegetable soup, roll, glass of water"—
without pocketing a few cellophane-wrapped crackers
            "for later."

At six, I got my first lesson in thrift.
Grandpa with a smoker's cough:
"Cough into four corners of hanky,
like this—
four coughs minimum—,
before you dirty up the middle."
End of lesson.

3. *His curses*

Late summer afternoons, partaking of Mogen David
("Shield of David") wine,
he orbited the living room, sonofabitching
the government
                          and Democrats with no sense,
Franklin and Eleanor Roosevelt, "betrayers of the rich,
and they stole my patent, too."

God damning union leaders, "schnorrers,"
the United Mine Workers,
the AFL and CIO,
"Stand 'em up against a wall.
Shoot 'em, shoot the sons-a-bitches."

4. *His secret to health and long life*

Old Testament Moses,
cigarette and drink in hand,
white mustache, gray beard, pacing, pacing,
"God" (it was a prayer after all),
"damn" (the patriarch calling down wrath),
"son-a-bitch, son-a-bitch."
The last of his great inventions,
five syllables to God's four ("Let there be light"),
but good enough.
And that is how he'd breathe, cursing
—head back, chin up—everyone who, he figured,
had somehow cost him money.
"God damn son-a-bitch, God damn son-a-bitch!" he'd rage,
miraculously cured of whatever ailed him.

THE BIGGEST PARTY ANIMAL OF THEM ALL

The biggest party animal of them all
spoke Hindi, a little English,
suffered from diabetes,
     was allergic to incense,
flowers and perfume,

loved chocolate,
     gave it away, used it as *prasad*,
a gift to his disciples.

In his 70s he gave himself away,
reportedly 'poking' as many as 300
of his youngest followers.

'Now's your chance,' he'd say, his mouth full.
'That's right, child. Lie back,
meditate,' he'd croon. 'Have faith.'

The dude separated so many people from so much money
he had to create the Guru Om Foundation.
Rolls Royces, chauffeurs, ashrams in all the major cities.

The movement started small, twenty,
     thirty,
          then hundreds,
               soon—

     doctors, lawyers,
hoteliers, cocaine dealers and professors,
          dancers, artists
and musicians

     flocked to him,
himself a musician, masked actor, comic,
     storyteller
          extraordinaire.

               Flatulent, potbellied old mystic,

giver-away of toys, party hats and favors to devotees.
The 'hundred-hatted yogi' we called him.

God, he was fun to be around!

Festivals with world-renowned performers,
dinner for five thousand,

                                    and, afterwards,
we got to approach and touch his feet.

True, sometimes he'd flip out, become enraged,
have to be strapped down
or held,
            one devotee at each limb.
Rudra the Howler.

Then, reviving,
'Chant.' 'Dance.' 'Meditate.'
Nataraj, the dancing Shiva, O graceful one!

Once, mid-revelry, irked by something I'd read aloud,
he drew back, swatted me four, five times
with a mass of peacock feathers. Whoosh! Whoosh!

It's known as 'Shaktipat,' kick-start Kundalini yoga,
where the party thrower has only to touch someone—
blow to the head or soft caress—

and Zap!

For two, maybe three, minutes
I saw two worlds interpenetrating

jewels into jewels,
silver suns, electric whiteness,

World 'A' and world 'B'
one vibrating blue pearl,

world like a skyful of blue suns
Whoosh! Whoosh! Whoosh!

Head spinning, I began to laugh,
and he too, old cobra face,
        began to howl,

mister three in one. Mister one in three.

O thou paunchy one
      in Birkenstocks
           and orange silk robe, trickster,
magician,
      master cocksman,
hit me again!

Seven years I hung out with him,
even flew to India, meditated
          in his cave
chanting to
      scorpions, malaria mosquitoes
so illumined they chanted back.

        phallic god,
        god in the shape of a dick,
           godfather
           con man

        killer god, god of death
        and destroyer of all life

        'Sonofabitch,' I say
        'Sonofabitch!'
        The guests are still arriving,
        the party's just begun.
                    —Oakland, California

FASHION MAKES THE HEART GROW FONDER

"Marriage and hanging go by destiny."
—Robert Burton, Anatomy of Melancholy

Partygoers
Her fruity, floral fragrance—
Honey at her dressing table
        like a pilot in the cockpit,
a woman armed with old TV Guides, catalogs,
ordering information
        for all the major scents and potions.

She put on (how can I describe them?)
refrigerator avocado green
        and white
Keith Partridge bell bottoms. Incandescent,
no less bizarre, I wore purple velveteen pants
and a tie-dyed shirt.

Her old lover Warren was there in his pimp suit,
        giant bug-eye sunglasses
and huge fake fur pimp hat,
a party with vintage Joan Crawford movies,
Honey wearing Chanel Number 5,
        the first synthetic scent.

And me, her consort, I wore
 'a blend of crisp citrus and warm spice, mossy woods, a scent
for the feeling man.'

I remember her silver and turquoise earrings
on the make-up table
as the bed jumped and jerked
those first two years.

Ravi Shankar, Thai weed, and a little homegrown,
that velvet ribbon choker with butterflies
and the scent of Honey when she dropped her
        tooled leather belt on the floor.

Then, "Tell me what you want," I said.
"You can't give me what I want."
"What do you want?"
"I'm out of style and so are you.
I want to lose weight."

And like that it was over.

"How about this handbag?" offered *Cosmo*,
"the perfect accessory
to the outfit you wear
when you leave your husband."

And that's how it ended. Honey at some fashion show
throwing back her head, the spotlight playing
on her face and neck.

Yes, I could see what Honey wanted,
to shop where she'd never shopped before,
to pull on high leather boots
and a mini-skirt; then, beaded Navaho handbag in hand,
flashing a little scented thigh, walking out on someone
who couldn't keep up,
a jerk in tie-dye.

I loved the woman, longed to stay with her and,
to do so, if I could have, arm-in-arm with her,
I'd have walked out on myself.

MY MUSE

*"As a rule, the power of absolutely falling in love soon vanishes...
because the woman feels embarrassed by the spell she exercises over
her poet-lover and repudiates it..."*
> —Robert Graves, The White Goddess

"Why don't you just write a poem, right now?" she says.
'Western wind, when wilt thou blow...'
why don't you write a poem like that,
like that 'Anonymous'? Something inspirational."

"Talk about muses," I sulk,
"Yeats' wife was visited in her dreams by angels
saying, 'We have come to bring you images
for your husband's poetry.'"

"Yeah? So what?" she says. "It's out of style.
I already do too much for you."

Odalisque in a wicker chair,
book open on her lap,
dry Chardonnay at her side,
hand on a dozing, whiskered Sphinx.

"You need a muse," she says, "someone beautiful, mysterious,
some long-lost love,

                    fragile, a dancer perhaps. Look at me..."

"Yeah?" I say, refilling her glass,
"You hear me complaining? You're *zaftig*."
             "Zaftig?"
        "Firm, earthy, juicy, too," I say.

        *   *   *

"Juicy plum," I say, in bed, left hand over her head,
"rose petals," I say, right arm around her.

"Silver drop earrings," I murmur, ordering out
for gifts. "Aubergine scarf, gray cashmere cardigan."

I do this in my sleep. Go shopping in my sleep.
"Oh, yeah, and a case of Chardonnay."
Wake to the scent of apple blossoms,
decades in the glow of roselight.

*   *   *

"Wake," she whispers. I tell her my dream.
We kiss. Poppy Express. Racy Red. Red Coral.
        Star Red.
                Red red.

        "Enough. That's enough," she says.

NIGHTGOWN, WIFE'S GOWN

Where do people go when they go to sleep?
I envy them. I want to go there too.
I am outside of them, married to them.
Nightgown, wife's gown, women you look at,
beside them—I knock on their shoulder blades
ask to be let in. It is forbidden.
But you're my wife, I say. There is no reply.
Arms around her, I caress her wings.

AMNESIA

Somewhere an ocean of doorknobs,
a cemetery for seaweed.

                                     The sailors,
                     all of them,
            walking
     at
some slight angle
counter to the angle
everyone else
walks at.
The ships and the rain
  slanting
    at still
      another
        angle.
And music
and the woman
one has children by
bears her child
and her belly
every day
at a different
angle.

We are under water
Come up and the surf is filled with rooftops, planes overhead
narrowly missing trees, it begins raining upwards.

Things get lonely to go outside.
Sometimes the body gets lonely to go outside.
Sometimes everything and the body also goes outside
                   at once.

Every morning at precisely that moment
the woman asks for his dreams,

he has none,
or forgets or wants to forget or
conceives he is dying.
In his memory
they break up
almost entirely
because he can not
remember his dreams.
On the other hand, she remembers hers
and tells them
compulsively.

He reads bedsheets. Imprint of lines. The woman's neck.
The word "Mother" tattooed somewhere. A cluster of red
freckles above the "M." She sits up and yawns.
"I want," she says, "I want."

THE HOUSE ON STILTS

Cross Lake, Wisconsin - Illinois   1950

There is no sleep, this night
in me, in the room
where I write my sleep.
I open the window, and unhook
the screen; the bushes, metal lawn chairs
      streetlamps
the moon, pieces of a livingroom.

Stilts, rotted long pilings,
stand just beneath the bookcase, TV,
bedroom and kitchen,
the four corners of the house.

    The sky,
a starry imitation ceiling–
our family, propped,
      house-on-stilts people,
goiter, bulgy-eyed mother,
    weekend father,
half in one state, half in
another
        dots and dashes on the map,
Cross Lake with a line
running through it.

      *   *   *

The highway alive, aloud
a blatant strip of rug.
    And people,
    in their houses,
    the back doors opening, slamming.

Every hour
someone screams quietly for a while.
And babies, in little closed windows.
The TV, a bluish, fluorescent hearth.

–Tilting, facing
                its double, the house on stilts.

A house in the shape, a dream
                in the shape, of itself
                of its house, of its dream.

                A sleep
the impossibility of sleep,
the vision, the life that it requires.
Her eyes opening, singing,
my mother, former Miss Chicago,
                on a springboard.

PRAYER FOR MY MOTHER

"May the Great Name be blessed..."

1. *Mother's Limousines*

"Mourn like a Jew," Grandfather says,
tearing my shirt
                    from the collar down,
"and when she's buried, rip out the grass
              and wail.
Expose your heart. Lament for her."

                    Mother, mother
                    mother of the inflamed heart.

Car door slamming behind us as we exit...

Bar-mitzvah'd boy, 13, I say it once,
say what I'm told to say,
"He is the Rock, His work is perfect..."
Say it,
                    YIT-GA-DAL
                    V'YIT-KA-DASH
                    SH'MEI
                    RA-BA
                    B'AL MA...
              the Kaddish of sounds, not words

"May a great peace from heaven..." I say,
"May His great Name be blessed,
...Magnified and sanctified...
                    Y'HAY
                    SH'LAMA
                    RA-BA
                    MIN SH'MAYA
                    V'CHAYIM
                    ALENU... I say.

...a week later,
      no to the rabbi,
      no to morning,
      no to twilight,
         no to the mid-day prayer
no repeating the prayer three times a day for a year
      no, I say, and no to the shul.

            "We're animals first and human second," she says,
            "and there is no God.

                      Do you hear me?"

Fox-trotting mother. Dancer mother. Beauty Queen
      in the house of prayer.

            "Mom," I ask, "how do you pray?"
            She shakes her head and turns away.
                  "Snap out of it," she says.

            "Better to go shopping," she says,
            "better to get a job, better to make money."
            I reach out. "Mom—"

            "Hands off," she says,
            "hands off."

            "Kids," she says. "Oy vay."
                "Holocaust," she says. "Oy oy, oy."
              "God," she says.
                  "What God?"
"Bless the Lord who is blessed," I don't pray.
"May the Great Name be blessed," I don't pray,
      but burn a candle so Mother,
Miss Chicago,
         can find her way back.

            Later, I cannot recall her face.
            "...you're not to look on any photo of her,

not for seven days," says Grandfather.
What did she even look like?
Faceless son
                mourning a faceless mother,
                mourning her,
        mourning
                freelance,
        mourning on the fly.

"She'll wander for seven days," Grandfather says,
"then, when she's wormed, her soul will return to God."

                lacks a body and I can't recall her face
                lacks a body and I can't recall her face

"Save her soul from Gehenna.
"Join us," pleads the rabbi.
                No, no is my prayer
No to duty and no to prayer.

Who was she? Some brunette rich girl
I never knew,
        a stranger dead at 42.
Mother, the beautiful secretary.
I touch her in a dream. She turns,
and there's no one there.

I shake from head to foot.
I stand and I sway.
"Mother, Mother," I say.

Blessed be the stranger.
No, no to the stranger,
no to the stranger.

No is my Kaddish.
No is my prayer.
I am the no

I am the not.

I will not be her savior,
I will not.

2. *Gehenna, or Purgatory*

       Mother applies Pond's Beauty Cream. Her face glistens.
       Massages her forehead with one hand,
       holds the other to her heart.

"What's the point?" she asks, cigarette ablaze,
       mouth tightening.

       When she dies, they bury her not in a shroud,
              but in pancake make-up
       and best gray dress.

"Turn the photos to the wall," says Grandfather,
"and cover your lips.

       That's right. Now cover your face.
Isolate yourself — groan — let your hair grow wild.
The mourner is the one without a skin, says the Talmud.
Understand? You are no longer whole."
And I think: *I am going to die, too.*

Sit in silence and say nothing.

       "How about a prayer to locusts?" I pray,
       "How about a prayer to boils?

       "O murdering heaven," I pray.

Grandfather cooks lentils,
lentils and eggs. "Mourners' food," he calls it.

       "A prayer to rats,
       and a prayer to roaches."
"Death is the mother of beauty," he says.
"The death of another makes you want to die," he says.

"The Angel of Death is made entirely of eyes," Grandfather says.

> Damn seeing,
> Damn touching.
> Damn feeling.
> Damn loving.

In Jewish hell—

> I am the unknowing,
> the not Jewish Jew.

Split, cloven,
       cracked

> In hell
>
> nameless,
> and eyeless,
>   faceless.
> No, no to blessings,
> no to teachings,
> no to reading from right to left.
>
> I pray with them,
> I pray with the no, I pray with the not.
> I pray with the dead, I pray with the damned.
>
> God, God who is a wound, we pray.

3. *Against Darkness*

> "Kaddish is a song against darkness," says the rabbi.
> YIT-GA-DAL
> V'YIT-KA-DASH
> SH'MEI
> RA-BA
> B'AL MA...
>
> > "'Magnified and sanctified
> > May His Great Name Be...'

"No it says, no to darkness. No to nothingness.
                'May His Great Name be blessed.'
"Kaddish praises God...
"Kaddish: a mourner's prayer
that never mentions death.
Y'HAY
SH'LAMA
RA-BA
MIN SH'MAYA
V'CHAYIM...

"Now then, Let E__, the son of G__,
                come forward," says the rabbi,
but I freeze, pretend not to hear.
Again he calls, calls me to say Kaddish.
(Loudly) "Let E__, son of G__, step beside me."
Ten other mourners turn in my direction.

Again I pretend not to hear.
Staring, face crimson, then white, he turns
                and continues with the service.

                "The Lord is our God, the Lord is One..."
I mourn her — mourn Kaddish — mourn shul
and head for home. Age 13, I walk out
                looking
                                for stones
I might hurl into heaven.

        *   *   *

                I am the un-bar'd mitzvah,
                escaped
                                Jew from nowhere,
                apostate,
                skipped Jew,
                                cleft Jew,
                Jew, pause in the beating of the heart.

        *   *   *

Once home, I pray, "Damn Him,
              "damn G-d," I pray.

              *   *   *

Mother, car door slamming,
              the shovel biting
Mother, whose body is the world,
              spinning into space—

"Life rattles," she says.
"My son, His Royal Highness," she says,
              "get used to it."

"Mom, is there an afterlife?"
"Shape up," she says. "You are my afterlife.
              God help us."

4. *Anniversary*

"We're just subdivisions of one person.
One's no better than any other.
Someone dies and you move forward
              into the front lines," Grandfather says,
                            lighting a yortzeit candle.

                            "'Blessed art thou who raises the dead...'"

Shaking the match, he turns. "Gottenyu!" he says.
"I should have been next."
Tears well up
              and I see him see her
                                          in me.

"Same color hair,
              same eyes..." Grandfather says.
"Remember seeing her in her coffin?" he asks,
              grabbing my arm.

"Your mother didn't believe, but she'll be raised
and rest with G-d. Does love quit?

"Can you feel her... hear her inside you?"
I nod.
"Where?"
"Here, in my chest."
"And what does she say?"
"She says nothing," I reply,
          but she does:

                    "Loopy doop," she says, "Rest in peace!
                    Wait'll you die, you'll see. There is no peace.
                         When you're dead,
                                   you're dead.
                         Enough.
                    Meshugge!" she says, and shakes her head.

"Pray, damn you," he says. "It's your mother."

"...Now it's over," he sobs.
          "But you, the un-mourner
will mourn for her all your life.

"Jew, Jew without beginning," he mocks,
"Jew who got away,
          sinner, sinner," he yells,
"snap out of it."

Books by Robert Sward

POETRY
Advertisements, Odyssey Chapbook Number One, 1958
Uncle Dog & Other Poems, 1962
Kissing The Dancer & Other Poems, Introduction by William Meredith, 1964
Thousand-Year-Old Fiancee, 1965
Horgbortom Stringbottom, I Am Yours, You Are History, 1970
Hannah's Cartoon, 1970
Quorum/Noah (With Mike Doyle), 1970
Gift, 1971
Five Iowa Poems, 1975
Cheers For Muktananda, 1976
Honey Bear On Lasqueti Island, B.C., 1978
Six Poems, 1980
Twelve Poems, 1982
Movies: Left To Right, 1983
Half-A-Life's History, Poems New & Selected, 1983
The Three Roberts, Premiere Performance, 1984
(Featuring Robert Priest, Robert Zend, and Robert Sward)
The Three Roberts On Love, 1985
The Three Roberts On Childhood, 1985
Poet Santa Cruz, Introduction by Morton Marcus, 1985
Four Incarnations, 1991
Uncivilizing. A Collection of Poems, 1996

FICTION
The Jurassic Shales, A Novel, 1975
Family, with contributions by David Swanger, Charles Atkinson, Tilly Shaw, 1994
A Much-Married Man, A Novel, 1996

NON-FICTION
The Toronto Islands, Illustrated History, 1983

EDITED BY ROBERT SWARD
Vancouver Island Poems, An Anthology, 1973
Emily Carr, Artist: The Untold Story, 1978